No. ______

In the Supreme Court of the United States

Samuel H. Sloan,
Administrator of Estate
of K. Michael Goodall
with Will Annexed
vs.
Bank of America N. A.,
James R. Hastings, and
Guide Dogs For the Blind, Inc.

On Petition for a Writ of Certiorari to the California Court of Appeal, First Appellate District, Division Four

---

PETITION FOR A WRIT OF CERTIORARI

Samuel H. Sloan
Administrator of Estate
of K. Michael Goodall
with Will Annexed
461 Peachstone Terrace
San Rafael CA 94903
(415) 419-5980
917-659-3397
samhsloan@gmail.com

AF810851

Questions Presented

Does the filing of a timely petition for discovery after the superior court judge abruptly decided this case without any discovery or hearing at all toll the time to file a notice of appeal until after the judge has signed the order denying the rehearing?

Did the actions of the superior Court judge in waiting two full months after the had denied the petition for rehearing from the bench but before he signed the order denying rehearing so as to deliberately put the case past the time to file a notice of appeal deprive the estate of the deceased and the heirs of the estate of due the constitutional right to process of law?

Did the actions of the San Francisco Superior Court judge in effectively taking this case away from the Marin County Probate Court which had appointed petitioner as administrator of the estate including the property which is located in Marin County violate the standard rule that all cases jurisdiction involving proceedings concerning real property must take place in the jurisdiction where the property was located which is Marin County?

Were the actions or lack thereof by the Judge of the Superior Court of the State of California in which he issued an abrupt ruling without any of the normal procedures, without any discovery being allowed, with no production of documents, no motion for summary judgment filed, no findings of fact and conclusions of law, no fact hearing of any kind, no declarations or statement of facts under oath and none of the recognized procedures for the conduct of any case having been followed constitute such as vast deviation of established legal practice as to constitute a violation of Constitutional Rights to Due Process of Law as guaranteed by the Fifth and Fourteenth Amendments to the Constitution of the United States?

When a petition in probate has been filed and has been granted by a superior court of a county, may a party be allowed to file a proceeding in some other county where none of the deceased ever lived in that other county, none of their property has ever been located in that other county, where the wills the deceased are all in probate in the first county and there is no connection with the second county of anything having anything to do with this case?

Table of Contents

Appendix

Exhibit A

Exhibit B
Declaration by supposed witness to the wills saying that she never witnessed any such wills

Exhibit C

Declaration by attorney James R. Hastings saying that he has lost the trust documents

Petition for a Writ of Certiorari

Petitioner Respectfully Prays that a Writ of Certiorari issue to the California Court of Appeal, First Appellate District, Division Four to review the decision of the California Court of Appeal dismissing this appeal on on January 15, 2013. Petition for Rehearing was denied on February 6, 2013. Case No. A137190. The California Supreme Court denied the Petition for Review on April 17, 2013. Case No. S208895

Parties to the Case

Bank of America N. A.
represented by
Gary D. Rothstein
Manatt, Phelps & Phillips, LLP
One Embarcadero Center, 30th Floor
San Francisco CA 94111

James R. Hastings, Esq.
1003 3rd Street
San Rafael, CA 94901
represented by

Don A. Lesser
1010 B Street
Suite 350
San Rafael CA 94901

Please note: Although Don Lesser states that he no longer represents James R. Hastings, both he and attorney James R. Hastings appeared in this case and has never filed a notice of withdrawal from this case.

Guide Dogs for the Blind
represented by
Alicia A. Adornato
Attorney for Guide Dogs for the Blind
Reed Smith LLP
101 Second Street, Suite 1800
San Francisco CA 94105

Constitutional Provisions Involved

The Fifth Amendment to the United States Constitution provides:

[N]or shall any person . . . be deprived of life, liberty, or property, without due process of law . . . .

Section One of the Fourteenth Amendment to the United States Constitution provides:

[N]or shall any State deprive any person of life,

liberty, or property, without due process of law . . . .

Table of Cases

There are no cases involved in this case. In none of the pleadings filed by Bank of America, by James R. Hastings or by Guide Dogs for the Blind have they ever cited a case or provided any legal authority supporting what they have done in this case or that they have standing to appear in this case or to request the relief they seek, which is to "donate" the Goodall Estate to Guide Dogs for the Blind without ever even giving an accounting or describing what is in the Goodall Estate.

OPINIONS BELOW

There are no opinions below. Neither the San Francisco Superior Court, nor the California Court of Appeal, First Appellate District, Division Four nor the California Supreme Court has issued any written or oral decision in this case.

Jurisdiction

The California Court of Appeal, First Appellate District, Division Four, dismissed this appeal on on January 15, 2013 with a summary order stating:

> "Appellant Samuel Sloan purports to appeal from a September 27, 2012 order denying his motion for reconsideration. A court's ruling

> on a motion for reconsideration is not appealable. (Code Civ. Proc. § 1008, subd. (g).) The appeal is dismissed."

Petition for Rehearing was denied on February 6, 2013. Case No. A137190.

The California Supreme Court denied the Petition for Review on April 17, 2013. Case No. S208895

However, the judge of the San Francisco Superior Court had waited two full months before signing the order submitted to him. The order was submitted to the judge for signing on July 27, 2012. The judge did not sign it until September 26, 2012 and it was entered the following day. This had put it beyond the appeal time. Case No. PTR-99-273030

http://webaccess.sftc.org/Scripts/Magic94/mgrqispi94.dll?APPNAME=IJS&PRGNAME=ROA22&ARGUMENTS=-APTR99273030

The parallel case in Marin County is Case No. PRO1100596

Statement of the Case

This case involves a 501(c)(3) charities scam which is extreme even as these charities scams go. The Form 990 filed by Guide Dogs for the Blind shows that they receive more than $30 million per year in donations and now have $307 million in net assets. They pay their directors more than one million dollars per year in salaries. They own more than one hundred houses in Marin County alone, making them the largest property owner in Northern California. They bring in their donations from two groups, dog lovers and those who want to help blind people. Guide Dogs for the Blind Inc. owns a hundred houses in Marin County and has 40 buildings on their campus, some under construction.

They do what almost all similar charities do, which is pressure wealthy people on their death beds to leave their estates to their charity rather than to their children. However, in the case here they have far gone beyond that by using forged signatures to gain property from those who never intended to give them anything.

On August 24, 1994, 17 days before Col. Kenneth Goodall died of Cancer of the Esophagus, Guide Dogs for the Blind claims that he signed documents giving them the right to the entire $2.5 million Goodall Estate.

However, as anybody can plainly see, the signatures are different. We hired a handwriting expert who looked at the signatures with a microscope. We also gave him a dozen other known signatures of the Goodalls from various dates.

Our handwriting expert, who also does this work for the FBI, immediately noticed substantial differences between the signatures, especially with the unusual way that Kenneth F. Goodall signed the FG of his name. Col. Kenneth F. Goodall always signed the FG of his signature with one sweeping stroke of the pen. His pen never left the paper.

Looking at the signature on the purported trust. It is a slow and halting signature and goes in the opposite direction from the way that Col. Goodall normally signed his name and is in three parts.

We can and will prove in court that Guide Dogs for the Blind and their nine attorneys are knowingly using forged instruments to steal a $2.5 million estate from the legitimate heirs.

The obviously forged signatures here are all taken from original documents on file with the San Francisco Probate Court, Case No. PTR-99-273030 and downloadable at http://webaccess.sftc.org/Scripts/Magic94/mgrqispi94.dll?APPNAME=IJS&PRGNAME=ROA22&ARGUMENTS=-APTR99273030

We can prove that the forger is attorney James R. Hastings were it not for the fact that Hastings says that he has lost the documents and thus refuses to produce them. Not only does he claim not to have the documents, he claims he does not even have a photocopy thereof, even though he drafted them. Bank of America claims not to have the documents either. So, according to Bank of America, they have been administering this estate under protest from the Goodall Family and the Goodall heirs, without ever having the documents upon which their claims are based, or indeed any documents at all.

Nowadays it seems that the papers are filled with allegations of misconduct by Bank of America in taking over properties and evicting people from their homes. Those cases usually involve mortgages. However, in this case no mortgage is involved. The Goodalls built their house with their own money and never borrowed from a bank. They never had a bank account with Bank of America, not even a simple checking account. The Goodalls notoriously mistrusted and hated attorneys. None of their documents make any mention of Bank of America or of Guide Dogs for the Blind, even though the drafting attorney, James R. Hastings, was the head of the Trust Department of the Bank of America at the time.

We can prove that the Goodalls never signed and could not have signed the key document which Bank of America says that Col. Goodall signed because he was hospitalized and on life support at that time and thus could not possibly have gone to the office of James R. Hastings in San Rafael to sign the documents. The highly regarded handwriting expert says that the FAXed copies (the only copies Bank of America has thus produced) are not consistent with known signatures of Col. Goodall. The supposed witness says that she did not sign them and those are not her signatures. Bank of America says that it has lost the documents and refuses to produce them. Bank of America also refuses to provide any accounting of the funds.

What we have here is a clear case of criminal theft by Bank of America and their attorneys of an estate involving $2.5 million, almost all of which has been consumed by attorney's fees by Bank of America. The evidence points to the conclusion that the key signatures were forged by James R. Hastings, who was the Trust Administration Attorney for the Trust Department of the Bank of America and who prepared and witnessed and notarized the documents in this case. In order to cover up these crimes, Bank of America wants to donate the entire estate to a charity, Guide Dogs for the Blind, leaving the actual Goodall heirs with nothing. The San Francisco Superior Court judge first wrongfully took jurisdiction over a case where there is no jurisdiction and then ruled in favor of Bank of America without allowing any discovery and with no fact hearing of any kind. The judge then made the case "Appeal Proof" by deliberately not signing the order denying rehearing until delaying two months to put it past the time to file a notice of appeal.

This case is running in parallel between two different courts in Marin and San Francisco, with opposite results. In the San Francisco case, the case is Case No. PTR 99-273030. In Marin County, the Case numbers are PRO1100596 and CV1204541.

Petitioner appeals herein from an order which denied a motion for Discovery. Please Note: The motion that Petitioner, who is the Administrator of the Estate of Michael Goodall with Will Annexed, filed on May 25, 2012 was NOT a motion for a rehearing of the May 16, 2012 order for the reason that petitioner believed and still believes that the May 16, 2012 was an interlocutory and therefore probably not appealable, since it did not finally decide the action. In addition, it could not be a motion for a rehearing because there was no hearing in the superior court. There was no sworn testimony, no declarations, no verifications, no evidence presented (because counsel for Bank of America said that the evidence had been lost). Thus, there was none of the things that normally accompany a judicial determination of facts.

The motion which Petitioner-appellant filed was entitled "MOTION TO COMPEL PRODUCTION OF DOCUMENTS AND FURTHER DESPOSITION AND DECLARATION OF SLOAN IN SUPPORT THEREOF."

The Grounds for this review are to secure uniformity of decisions from around the state because this case is running in parallel in two different courts and these two courts have reached the opposite decisions. They know about each other and refuse to change their rulings so review by an appellate court is necessary.

A motion for discovery under the circumstances of this case is or should be appealable precisely because there has never been any discovery in this case except for a deposition of James R. Hastings in which he testified that he could not remember anything about this case and had lost or misplaced all his files of this case and so he had nothing to produce.

However, it was the Superior Court Judge and the Opponents who said that this was a motion for reconsideration.

Review is necessary and appropriate because this case is running in parallel between two different courts in Marin and San Francisco, with opposite results. In the San Francisco case, the case is Case No. PTR 99-273030. In Marin County, the Case numbers are PRO1100596 and CV1204541.

In almost every instance, the issues in the San Francisco Case are exactly the same as the issues in the Marin Case, yet the results have been the opposite. For example, the Bank of America filed a Statute of Limitations Claim in the Marin case. Judge Verna Adams dismissed that claim in a reasoned and lengthy opinion on April 16, 2012. Undaunted, Bank of America filed exactly the same claim in San Francisco, which resulted in an order from which an appeal is taken here.

Similarly, The Bank of America took the ruling by the San Francisco Court here and tried to enforce it over in Marin in a motion for summary judgment. However, the Marin County Superior Court Judge denied the claim by Bank of America, saying that the San Francisco order was interlocutory and non-final and thus non-enforcable in Marin. The Marin County judge ruled that Bank of America must file a claim to quiet title in Marin since the property is in Marin. However, throughout the nearly three years that this litigation has been going on, Bank of America has been unwilling to submit its claims to the jurisdiction of the Marin courts, for reasons best known to Bank of America. This has resulted in this stalemate which will take action by the appellate courts to resolve.

Because of these conflicting decisions by different judges in different courts, the situation is in stalemate. The Goodall Estate consists of an estimated two million dollars in cash and securities plus a house known as "The Goodall Mansion" located at 461 Peachstone Terrace, San Rafael California 94903. Bank of America has the money, having stolen it back in 1999 which resulted in this case, PTR 99-273030, whereas the Estate of Goodall has possession and control of the house. Bank of America has been unsuccessful in its efforts to oust the Goodall Estate from the house.

In order for this court to conclude that this was a motion for reconsideration and therefore non-appealable even though the motion says that it is a motion for discovery, this court must conclude that the prior order dated May 16, 2012 was a judgment. However, that order clearly was NOT a judgment. It did not use the word "judgment". It did not finally decide the action. It left unopened and undecided almost every question about this case.

Indeed, the Bank of America moved to enforce this order over in Marin County Superior Court and Judge Roy Chernus there said that the May

16 order was NOT a final judgment and was interlocutory.

On January 15, 2013, The California Court of Appeal dismissed summarily the appeal in this complicated case without waiting for the normal record, briefs and argument. Petitioner therefore did not get a chance to present his arguments to this court.

Since this court had never seen the record of this appeal because the Superior Court never had time to transmit it, it could not have understood the complex issues in this case. As Judge Roy Chernus of Marin County Superior Court stated in a one of the related cases in Marin County, "this is not your usual garden variety type of action" because while this case has been pending in the San Francisco Probate Court the same case has been pending over in the Marin County Probate Court. Two courts have been handling the same case.

Plaintiff here, Bank of America, lost their initial motions over in Marin County and then opted for the greener pastures in San Francisco Probate Court. As this case has progressed, every time Bank of America lost a motion over in Marin County they filed the same motion in San Francisco where they won.

Regarding the statute of limitations claim that Bank of America made in an "Additional Reply" in which the Administrator of the Goodall Estate did not have a chance to respond, Bank of America had made exactly the same Statute of Limitations claim in Marin County and Judge Verna Adams had dismissed that claim in a reasoned and lengthy opinion on April 16, 2012. Undaunted, Bank of America made that identical claim on San Francisco Probate Court.

Petitioner was prevented by the actions of opposing counsel and actions of the judge which made it impossible for him to file the appeal any sooner than he did. Indeed, Petitioner waited in the court room for the San Francisco Judge to sign his final order in this case so he could go down to the filing room to file this notice of appeal.

In view of the actions of the San Francisco Probate Judge in making this case "Appeal Proof" by among other things waiting a full two months before signing the order denying the petition for rehearing the judge prevented an earlier appeal. The order was submitted to the judge for signing on July 27, 2012. The judge did not sign it until September 26, 2012.

More than that, actions by Bank of America and Guide Dogs for the Blind unethically to chase Petitioner's Counsel off the case made it impossible for Petitioner to retain new counsel. They did this by repeatedly filing motions for sanctions against existing counsel. Their first motion for sanctions which demanded attorneys fees of $13,000 against both the Administrator of the Goodall Estate and his counsel was filed on June 29, 2012. That motion was denied by Judge Busch on June 19, 2012.

However, on the very next day, July 20, 2012,

Bank of America filed a second motion for sanctions even though nothing had changed overnight since the first denial.

A Third Motion for Sanctions was filed by Bank of America on August 14, 2012.

All these motions for sanctions filed by a big and powerful Bank of America and their counsel one of the largest law firms in California had the effect of understandably frightening the counsel for the Goodall estate. As no man can serve two masters, Counsel for the Goodall estate felt that he had to withdraw as counsel for the estate in order to defend himself against these successive motion for sanctions which threatened his professional career.

Meanwhile, Sam Sloan, the Administrator of the Goodall Estate, the Petitioner here, found it impossible to retain another counsel because every other attorney is afraid of Bank of America and their attorney too.

As a result, Petitioner had no choice but to wait until these motions for sanctions and motion to withdraw were decided before he could file this notice of appeal. Petitioner was literally waiting in the courtroom for the judge to sign these orders so he could run down to the clerk's office and file this notice of appeal the same day.

After considering this matter, this court should dismiss this case entirely. The proper Probate Proceeding involving the Goodall Estate is now pending over in Marin County Probate Court.

Case No. PR 1100596. The Goodall wills are admitted into probate in Marin. Everything about this case happened over in Marin. The only reason Bank of America filed in San Francisco is they do not like the judge over in Marin.

In addition, Bank of America should not have been allowed to use the case number of this inactive case to file a new claim for a different cause of action. There was no activity in this case for 11 years from March 2000 to April 2011. This case should have been dismissed for inactivity under California Code of Civil Procedure Section 583.410. Thus this case should be dismissed with all orders vacated and Bank of America should be directed to file their claims in the right court, which is Marin County Probate Court.

We believe that the May 16, 2012 order is not a final judgment. It does not contain the word "Judgment". It does not include findings of fact and conclusions of law. It does not award money or property to anybody. It does not finally decide the action.

However, the orders of the San Francisco Court cannot be ignored because Bank of America claims that it is a judgment and they have moved to enforce it as a judgment.

In August and October, 2012 Bank of America filed two unlawful detainer actions in Marin County seeking to evict the Goodall heirs from the Goodall Mansion at 461 Peachstone Terrace San Rafael, California. These actions were unsuccessful, for the same reason Petitioner has stated from the beginning. Judge Chernus wrote:

> As against Sam Sloan and Kayo Kimura plaintiff seeks judgment for possession based on orders of the San Francisco Superior Court and the July 27, 2012, Sixty-day notice. Plaintiff has put its title to the property "at issue" in this unlawful detainer proceeding. The bulk of the allegations in the Complaint and the "Undisputed Facts" in support of the subject motion for summary judgment are addressed to plaintiffs extensive efforts by way of collateral proceedings in San Francisco Superior Court to confirm that the premises is an asset of the Trust for Michael created under the Goodall Trust dated September 12,1990, that title to the premises is in Bank America as trustee, and that plaintiff may administer the premises pursuant to the terms of Trust.
>
> Yet despite plaintiffs extensive allegations detailing the San Francisco proceedings, plaintiff does not actually allege or demonstrate via undisputed facts that the orders of the SF Sup. Court are final or that the issue of its title to the subject property has been fully and finally determined.
>
> Plaintiff appears to base its right to commence this unlawful detainer proceeding upon the Minute Order of the SF Superior Court dated July 19, 2012,

denying defendant's petition for reconsideration as plaintiff served the subject 60-Day Notice eight days later on July 27,2012, even though the court's order was not formally entered until September 27, 2012. (See Complaint, par. 19, and Exh. E) Even assuming the order denying defendant's petition for reconsideration constitutes a final and binding determination of plaintiffs title (though not specifically alleged) plaintiff served the 60-day notice before that order was formally entered on September 27, 2012. This unlawful detainer action was filed a mere 12-days later on October 9, 2012. As stated by the Court in Greenhut v. Wooden {1982} 129 Cal.App.3d 64,68, this is not your usual garden variety type of unlawful detainer action where the issue of title is strictly limited. Having put its own title in issue and by relying on the San Francisco Trust proceeding as the source of its authority to commence this proceeding plaintiff should demonstrate that title to the property has, in fact, been finally adjudicated in its favor. Plaintiff's pleading and evidence falls short of demonstrating a final adjudication of title in its favor and raises a question of fact whether the alleged 60-day notice was served prematurely.

As to defendants Hoppe and Thornally, a complaint for unlawful detainer must allege that the tenant continues in

> possession of the premises. (CCP $1161.) No cause of action for unlawful detainer exists if the tenant has quit before the action is filed. Defendants Hoppe and Thornally have filed answers admitting they have relinquished possession of the premises. In its motion, plaintiff claims that while Hoppe and Thornally have relinquished physical possession of the premises, "plaintiff is informed that Hoppe and Thornally have not relinquished their alleged right to possession of the premises." If a landlord wishes to determine rights to possession but not physical possession, it cannot do so by way of summary unlawful detainer; a quiet title action would be the proper remedy.

Thusly, Judge Chernus stated in essence the same thing petitioner Sloan has been saying from the first pleading which is that the only way for Bank of America to get what it wants is to file an action in Marin County. Bank of America can never succeed in obtaining access to real property in Marin by bringing a case in San Francisco.

This action by Bank of America should be dismissed and thrown out of court for a deeper reason, which is that Bank of America has never had standing in this case. Bank of America was never the legal trustee of the Goodall Trust. Kenneth and Rachel Goodall were the trustees. Upon the death of Kenneth, the Trust documents show that Michael became the co-trustee with his mother and upon her death Michael became the sole trustee. The documents showing this are annexed as exhibits here. At no time did Bank of America have any rights in this case. They simply usurped and stole this case because of the millions of dollars involved.

What happened is Bank of America stole the money, pure and simple. They have no right and no claim to the Goodall assets.

In addition, Guide Dogs for the Blind has no standing and no claim. The trust document upon which Bank of America and Guide Dogs for the Blind relies (although they have failed and refused to produce it and claimed to have lost it) does not establish their right.

Paragraph 6, note 1 of the petition filed by Bank of America contains the following noteworthy statement.

"The Provisions of the Bypass Trust are somewhat unclear with respect to the proper beneficiaries of the Trust for Michael in the wake of Mike Goodall's Death."

"Somewhat unclear" is a massive understatement or misstatement. The trust documents have been shown to several attorneys specializing in such matters. All them say that the trust documents are nonsense. "Absurd", "ridiculous" and several other adjectives are used to describe these trust documents. A well known San Francisco attorney says that the attorney who drew up this trust should be disbarred for incompetence.

On January 15, 2013, The California Court of Appeal dismissed summarily the appeal in this complicated case without waiting for the normal record, briefs and argument. Petitioner therefore did not get a chance to present his case to this court.

Michael Goodall died on October 5, 2010 in his home known as "The Goodall Mansion" at 461 Peachstone Terrace in San Rafael, Marin County, California. Petitioner found the Goodall Will among his papers and filed it in Marin County Probate Court in January 2011. On February 1, 2011, Petitioner filed a petition in probate. After consents were obtained from all of the heirs of the Goodall Estate, petitioner petitioned and after two hearings was appointed administrator of the estate.

Petitioner had the key to the house, as he has been a resident of the house. However, on February 28, 2011, while petitioner was away for a few days, there was a break-in and burglary in the house. The entire contents of the house was removed including all legal papers and documents of the Goodalls. When the burglary was discovered, 911 was called and this was reported as a burglary. Deputy Anthony Savas of the Marin County Sheriff's Department responded to the call. Deputy Savas said that he had been patrolling the area during the previous days and had observed a large trash dumpster in front of the house with a Spanish guy bringing stuff out of the house and putting it in the dumpster. However, Deputy Savas had not stopped to inquire, as this had seemed to be a routine case of somebody moving out.

After discovering that the Goodall Mansion had been burgled, the contents removed and the locks on the doors changed, Petitioner as well as heirs of the Goodall Estate searched for several weeks for the stolen Goodall stuff. Finally, by chance it was located in an Auction House in Alameda. The auction House identified Hamilton Kipp as the person who had brought the Goodall Estate stuff to the auction house. It was later established that Hamilton Kipp is an employee of Bank of America. Hamilton Kipp in turn had been told to break into the house and take all the stuff by James R. Hastings, a Marin County Estate Planning Attorney.

Petitioner filed an 850 Motion in Marin County Probate Court to recover estate property, namely the Goodall Stuff that had been taken by Hamilton Kipp. After two hearings before the Marin County Probate Judge, in June, 2011, Bank of America was forced to return the Goodall Stuff.

However, in the meantime, on April 21, 2011, Bank of America by way of collateral attack had filed a petition in San Francisco Superior Court seeking essentially to overturn the Marin County Probate Order which had listed among other things the Goodall Mansion as an asset of the Goodall Estate. In filing this new petition, Bank of America had used an old case number, PTR 99-273030. That was the number of a case Michael Goodall had filed in December 21, 1999 shortly after his mother had died in which he has sought the removal of Bank of America as Trustee on many grounds including the grounds that Bank of America was not the bank named in the Trust documents and that the proper trustee was Michael Goodall himself and if not himself then at least some bank not openly hostile to him as Bank of America was.

That 1999 case had never been finally decided because after a hearing Mike Goodall had run out of money to the fight the case and because Bank of America was using the funds in the Goodall Estate to fight him. The attorneys for Bank of America told him that if he did not stop fighting the case then the entire estate would be exhausted in attorneys fees and he would be left with nothing.

The attorneys for Bank of America have also been making the same statement in the current branch of the case, but this threat is less effective now because the Attorneys for Bank of America can and perhaps already have striped away all of the assets of the Goodall Estate, so there will be nothing left for the heirs anyway.

An attorney for Bank of America has informed one of the Goodall Heirs there is no money left in the estate. However, when Rachel Goodall died in June 1999 there was approximately one million dollars in the Goodall Estate plus the Goodall Mansion was worth an estimated $700,000. So, if truly the money is entirely gone that means that Bank of America has consumed the entire one million dollars in administration and attorneys fees. However, they must keep fighting this case because if they lose this appeal they will have to pay back the entire one million, plus interest.

The Living Trust set up by Kenneth and Rachel Goodall back in 1990 makes Michael Goodall the beneficiary of the trust. He also becomes the successor trustee of the trust if one or both of his parents dies. The only way a bank becomes a trustee is if Mike is declared incompetent by a court of competent jurisdiction. No such thing has happened.

The 1990 Trust names Security Pacific Bank as the Trustee. In a hearing on November 28, 2012 in Marin Superior Court, counsel for Bank of America said that Bank of America had become Trustee because:

> First, Security Specific Bank became Bank of America back in 1991. We were the successor. You'll probably take judicial notice of it, but that was a very big transaction.

See Transcript of the hearing of November 28, 2012 page 13 which is part of the record of this appeal.

However, this is not what happened. What happened was in 1992 Bank of America NT&SA purchased the assets of Security Pacific Bank. Then in 1998 Nations Bank in North Carolina purchased the assets of Bank of America NT&SA. Subsequently Nations Bank changed its name to Bank of America Corporation, which is a bank holding company located in Charlotte, North Carolina. Thus, the Bank of America today is a completely different entity from either Security Pacific Bank or Bank of America NT&SA. The operations headquarters of Bank of America is in Dallas Texas. It has no operations in California. This issue was raised by Mike Goodall's attorney, Rothman, when he filed this case back in 1999 pointing out that Bank of America today is not in any way the same bank as Bank of America back in 1990.

Counsel for Bank of America must be claiming that the two purchases of the assets of another bank in the 1992 and 1998 transactions also included the purchase of the "right" to be the successor Trustee to the Goodall Trust. It will take a review of the documents involved in these corporate transactions to determine if the purchase of the assets included the purchase of the right to be the successor trustee. However, none of this is of any moment because the January 1999 Amendment to the Goodall Trust, namely the Second Amendment to the Goodall Trust, makes Mike Goodall the co-trustee along with his mother. Thus, when Rachel Goodall died in June 1999 Michael Goodall survived as the sole trustee and Bank of America never became the legal trustee.

Bank of America knows this because an attorney for Bank of America drafted the Second Amendment to the Goodall trust.

Page 18 of a trust document, which Bank of

America claims is controlling, but which we are prepared to prove was never signed by any of the Goodalls, contains the following provision:

> "(d) If MICHAEL does not survive the surviving settler and leaves no issue who survive the surviving settler, the trustee shall distribute the trust property twenty thousand dollars ($20,000) to each of the then living brothers and sisters of the trustor RACHEL A. Goodall and the remainder to GUIDE DOGS FOR THE BLIND OF MARIN, INC., of San Rafael California."

The problem is that this provision only applies if Michael dies BEFORE his parents do. However, Mike survived his parents by 11 years. Kenneth F. Goodall was born 01 Mar 1916 and died 10 Sep 1994 at age 78. His Social Security Number was 444-40-8884. Rachel A. Goodall was born 23 May 1916 and died 07 Jun 1999. Her Social Security Number was 359-07-1738. Kenneth Michael Goodall was born 13 Jan 1946 and died 05 Oct 2010. His Social Security Number was 559-70-3352.

Since Mike Goodall died 11 years after his parents did, that paragraph does not apply. More than that, nowhere in the entire documents, 40 pages long, is there any mention of what happens if Mike dies after his parents do, except that the trust documents state that the trust is "dissolved" after the death of Mike Goodall.

This provision and the entire document makes it completely 100% clear that the Goodall Estate belongs entirely to Mike Goodall and his heirs, unless Mike Goodall dies before his parents do. There is no possible way that Guide Dogs for the Blind gets anything out of the Goodall Estate. Under no interpretation of the Goodall Trust does Guide Dogs for the Blind get anything.

Yet, Bank of America, in its initial petition filed in San Francisco Superior Court, said that it was due to drafting errors that the trust documents mistakenly do not give any money to Guide Dogs for the Blind. Bank of America asked the Superior Court to in effect rewrite the trust documents so as to give the Goodall Estate to the Dogs.

At the first hearing in San Francisco Superior Court on May 25, 2011, Petitioner appeared in pro per because he felt it absurd and ridiculous that Bank of America would file their petition, because the trust documents clearly DO NOT give any part of the Goodall Estate to the Dogs and secondly because this case was already pending as a probate case in Marin County that clearly had jurisdiction. The Goodalls all lived and died in Marin County, all of their property including their house was in Marin County, all their documents were executed in Marin County and there was nothing about this case that had anything to do with San Francisco County. Thus, San Francisco County obviously does not have jurisdiction. Petitioner expected that the San Francisco Court would throw the case out immediately.

In addition, Guide Dogs for the Blind is behind all

of the other heirs. The trust provides that each of the Goodall siblings gets $20,000. Rachel Goodall had five siblings, three brothers and two sisters, and Kenneth Goodall had two brothers. Many of them are dead but they all married and had children, some of whom were adopted. There are about twenty Goodall heirs listed on the service list and they all have the right to contest this case. Clearly, only the Marin County Probate Court has the jurisdiction, venue and competence to decide these claims.

In addition, the direct heirs of Michael Goodall may have a claim. The trust provides that his wife and/or children inherit from the trust.

Guide Dogs for the Blind are at the bottom of the totem pole. This case goes to the dogs and they get money only after all these other people and even then the Dogs do not get anything unless Michael dies before either of his parents do, which did not happen.

Because of all these factors, Petitioner did not take seriously the petition filed by Bank of America in San Francisco. Petitioner assumed that the San Francisco case would either be dismissed or else transferred to the right court, which was Marin County Probate Court.

Petitioner was thus shocked when the San Francisco judge with a wave of the hand and without giving any reason for the decision or indeed without saying anything at all ruled in favor of Bank of America and signed an order that had been handed up without even allowing the

Petitioner to see and comment on the order that was being signed.

Petitioner then realized that he had better retain counsel. After a long search, Petitioner found a qualified attorney willing to represent the Goodall Estate on a Contingency Fee basis. This was necessary because Bank of America had already taken all the money. The Goodalls had never had an account with Bank of America, not even a simple checking account. Col. Goodall was retired military officer, so most of the Goodall money was with USAA Investment Management in San Antonio, Texas. There were also smaller amounts with mutual finds and stock trading accounts. None of this was with Bank of America or anywhere in the state of California.

Right after Rachel Goodall had died in June 1999, Bank of America through its attorney James R. Hastings had contacted USAA Investment Management and directed that all Goodall funds be transferred to Bank of America. Mike Goodall had not been told about this and had no idea that this had happened. In short order, all of the bank accounts that Mike Goodall had been operating were stripped of their assets. Mike Goodall was left destitute and without funds. That is the reason why he filed this case on December 21, 1999.

Bank of America completely stonewalled, as they continue to do this day. They refused and still continue to refuse to give Mike Goodall or indeed any of the Goodalls any accounting or any information about what happened to the Goodall Millions. It was as if the funds had disappeared into a Black Hole.

Just before Kenneth Goodall died in 1994 he had an accounting done of the funds. The accounting shows that the Goodalls had very slightly less than one million dollars in cash and securities plus the fully paid for house. Rachel Goodall was an excessively frugal person. She basically never spent money on anything, so the money should at least have doubled since 1994.

It is important at all times to remember that this case is running in parallel in two different courts: San Francisco Superior Court and Marin County Probate Court. Obviously, the Marin County Court is the right court and at each hearing in San Francisco Petitioner has demanded transfer of this case to Marin.

At the next hearing in San Francisco, Bank of America brought attorney James R. Hastings to court prepared to have him testify as a witness as he had been attorney for both the Goodalls, the Goodall Trust and the Bank of America. Hastings was going to testify that the money should go to the Dogs. This was one of just many obvious conflicts on interest by James R. Hastings. However, Petitioner's new counsel Sam Ware asked for the opportunity of discovery. Bank of America protested vehemently and said that there should be no discovery at all. They especially objected to any discovery of the money. They refused to reveal anything about the Goodall millions, how much it was, were they had gotten it from and what they had done with it.

Finally, Judge Mary Wiss agreed that there should be some discovery. Whereas Bank of America wanted to hold a hearing and finish the case that day, the superior court judge said that there should be discovery.

However, as will be seen there has never been any discovery on this case, because Bank of America has been completely stonewalling. Not one document has been produced either by Bank of America or attorney James R. Hastings. Bank of America has absolutely refused to produce anything. James R. Hastings has testified that he has lost the files and thus does not have anything. In addition he has stated that to provide any discovery would violate the attorney Client Privilege of Bank of America because he was counsel for Bank of America at the same time that he was counsel for the Goodalls.

Sam Ware then subpoenaed James R. Hastings for a deposition and required him to bring all documents and files pertaining to this case. Hastings appeared for the deposition on November 14, 2011 but did not bring any documents at all. His attorney Don Lesser said that the subpoena was overbroad and as Hastings had been attorney for Bank of America too it would violate the attorney client privilege of Bank of America and that the files and notes pertaining to this case had all been lost. At the oral deposition, Hastings testified that basically he could not remember anything about the case.

On December 14, 2011 Sam Ware filed a motion for discovery and production of documents pertaining to this case.

On December 29, 2011, Don A. Lesser, Counsel for James Hastings, filed opposition to the motions for discovery, saying that it would be "oppressive and burdensome" upon James R. Hastings and also violate the attorney client privilege of Bank of America because James R. Hastings had been attorney for Bank of America at the same time that he was attorney for the Goodall and the Goodall Trust.

Not long thereafter Don Lesser withdrew as counsel for James R. Hastings.

On January 20, 2012, Judge Busch denied the motion for production of documents, especially the trust Document, but said that James R. Hastings was required to search his files to look for the trust and if he could find it he was required to produce it and otherwise he must file a declaration stating what efforts he had made to find the trust.

On February 2, 2012, James R. Hastings filed a declaration stating that he had searched all his files and was unable to find the trust.

On February 6, 2012, Nancy Rodgers, a friend and neighbor of the Goodalls, filed a declaration stating that her purported signatures on the Goodall Wills, which were pour over wills pouring money into the trust, were not her signatures and she had never signed such a document. As there had never been any money in the trust, these pour over wills were essential to the claims by Bank of America and Guide Dogs for the Blind to be entitled to any of the Goodall millions.

After several more pleadings were filed on all sides, on April 24, 2012, Bank of America filed an additional reply asserting for the first time in this case that objections to the 1994 Trust were time-barred by a Statute of Limitations. Although this was the first time Bank of America had made this claim in this case, they had made exactly the same claim in the parallel proceeding going on in Marin County Probate Court. That claim had been dismissed by Marin County Probate Judge Verna Adams in a lengthy and reasoned decision on April 16, 2012. The statute of limitations claim was also entirely bogus for several reasons the most obvious being that Michael Goodall had indeed contested the right of Bank of America to be the trustee by filing this very case on December 21, 1999. Also, the statute of limitations claim was not accompanied by any evidence or a declaration in support. In addition, the words "as amended" had been omitted or when it was included, obviously it logically referred to the 1999 Amendment to the Trust which had made Mike Goodall the Trustee. The 1990 Trust had made Michael Goodall the beneficiary of the trust and the 1999 Amendment had made Michael the co-trustee of the trust, so there was no reason for Michael to object to either of them.

Because of the shortness of time before the previously scheduled hearing, Samuel Sloan and his counsel did not have time to respond to this "additional reply" and so asked for additional time which was denied from the bench. And so, Judge Busch signed the order dated May 16, 2012 from which the first appeal is taken, without a fact hearing of any kind and without any findings of fact or conclusions of law.

On May 25, 2012, seven days after the entry of the order of May 16, 2012, Samuel Sloan filed through counsel a motion for discovery to compel the production of documents including the documents forming the basis of the newly made statute of limitations claim. This was not filed as a motion for reconsideration, because Sloan through counsel deemed the May 16, 2012 order to be an interlocutory order, not a final judgment, because, among many other things it does not use the word "judgment", and does not dispose of all of the issues involved in this case. However, this motion was filed within the time limit for motions for reconsideration to be on the safe side in case the courts were later to decide that it was a judgment.

Sam Sloan, Administrator of the Goodall Estate, had been caught off guard by the May 16, 2012 decision because he had naturally assumed that there would be some sort of trial or fact hearing and Bank of America would be required to present their evidence if any before the court would rule. It was not to be expected that the judge would decide this complicated case abruptly from the bench without any hearing. Because of this surprise ruling, the administrator started searching through the 40 or 50 storage boxes of material Bank of America had stolen when they broke into the Goodall Mansion on February 28, 2011 but then were forced to return on June 10, 2011 by proceedings in the Marin County Probate Court.

During these searches, the administrator found a treasure trove of documents. All or almost all of these documents had been prepared by James R. Hastings, Attorney for Bank of America, so Bank of America had these documents all along but had failed to produce them. Of great importance was a Power of Attorney the Goodall Parents, Kenneth and Rachel Goodall, had given their son Michael on August 24, 1994 on the Death Bed of Kenneth, placing Michael with power of attorney over the Goodall Trust. This proved that the claim by the Attorney of Bank of America that the Goodall parents did not trust Michael with their money was false. Also included in the same treasure trove of documents was a signed health care directive by Kenneth Goodall that he be allowed to die of the Esophageal cancer of which he was suffering at the time and an unsigned 1994 Goodall Trust showing that Kenneth had never signed the 1994 amendment to the trust. Kenneth Goodall was in the final stages of cancer and a feeding tube had been inserted in his abdomen on July 17, 1994. He died on September 10, 1994. These documents were included in the exhibits Sloan filed in his May 25, 2012 motion.

On the same date, Sloan filed a declaration of David S. Moore, a highly regarded forensic document examiner, who stated that upon comparing the known and authentic signatures of Kenneth Goodall found on other documents, on checks, on his personal notebook and the like and comparing them with the signature on the purported 1994 amendment to the trust, they were not consistent but he could not made a final determination as to whether the signature was authentic or not without being allowed to examine the actual trust document, but such an examination had been denied.

On June 27, 2012, Gary Rothstein, attorney for Bank of America served on Sam Sloan and his counsel Sam Ware a motion for sanctions against the Motion for Discovery dated May 25, 2012 asking for sanctions against Sam Sloan personally and against Sam Ware personally in the amount of $13,000 for filing the motion for discovery which they deemed to be a motion for reconsideration. In a cover letter, Gary Rothstein, attorney for Bank of America, stated that unless the motion for reconsideration were withdrawn he would file the motion for sanctions, effectively blackmailing the Goodall Estate.

It is important to remember here that Sloan is a volunteer administrator of the trust because the Goodall Trust has no money because Bank of America stole it all and Sloan is not named in the will. In addition, Attorney Sam Ware took this case as a contingency case. By serving this motion for sanctions Bank of America was threatening

Sloan and his counsel with a substantial financial loss whereas they had nothing to gain from this case.

So, the Administrator of the Goodall estate had everything to lose and nothing to gain by continuing this case.

On June 29, 2012 Guide Dogs for the Blind joined this motion by filing their own motion for sanctions for filing this petition for rehearing.

Nevertheless, the administrator and his counsel did not Cave in yet.

A hearing was held on these motions on July 19, 2012. Judge Busch denied the motion which he deemed to be a motion for reconsideration and he also denied the motion by Bank of America and Guide Dogs for the Blind for Sanctions against the Administrator of the Goodall Estate and Sam Ware, Counsel for the Goodall Estate.

On July 20, 2012, the very next day, Bank of America filed a new motion for Sanctions against the Administrator of the Goodall Estate and against Sam Ware Counsel for the Goodall Estate seeking sanctions in the amount of $13,000 against each of them. This motion had been denied from the bench the previous day so obviously nothing had changed.

On July 27, 2012, the parties submitted for the judge's signature an order denying the motion for reconsideration heard on July 19, 2012. Sam Sloan, Administrator of the Estate, planned and intended to file a notice of appeal as soon as the order was signed. Instead the judge sat on the order for two full months and did not sign in until September 26, 2012. It was entered the following day. This delay of two months put it past the normal time for filing a notice of appeal.

On August 14, 2012, Bank of America filed a third Motion for Sanctions against the Administrator of the Goodall Estate and his attorney.

On September 7, 2012, as a result of having three successive motions for sanctions filed against him, Sam Ware filed a motion to be relieved as counsel. He said that he could not effectively oppose the repeated motions for sanctions against him while also acting as counsel for the estate. No man can serve to masters so he needed to be relieved as counsel so that he could defend himself against actions by Bank of America and their counsel which threatened his professional career.

Now again Sloan could not file his notice of appeal because he had to wait until the judge decided the motion for sanctions and the motion by his counsel to withdraw to escape the sanctions. As Sloan was represented by Counsel he could not file the Notice of Appeal by himself. In addition, as these motions affected the merits of the case and the judge was retaining jurisdiction over the case there remained the possibility that the judge would reverse himself and the case would continue.

Finally, the judge held his hearing on the motion

to withdraw which was strenuously opposed by Sloan and granted the motion on November 15, 2012. On the same day, Judge Busch held his hearing on the motion for sanctions and denied that motion, basically saying that there was enough grounds for Counsel for the Goodall Estate to file a motion for reconsideration but not enough grounds for him to grant it.

On September 21, 2012, Judge Busch signed the order denying the Motion for Sanctions. Sloan filed his notice of appeal the very same day.

Reasons for Granting the Writ

The Court of Appeal dismissed the first appeal as untimely. Petitioner contends that it was not untimely because of the inappropriate and indeed unethical actions of both opposing counsel and the Superior Court judge. Opposing counsel kept filing motions even after the order appealed from. They filed three successive motions for sanctions in the amount of more than $13,000 against Petitioner and his counsel. It is important that Petitioner is a unpaid volunteer administrator because there is no money in the Goodall Estate and trust as Bank of America stole all the money. Petitioner is also not an heir to the Goodall estate. However, the real heirs to the Goodall Estate are depending on Petitioner to win this case because if Bank of America wins the heirs will get nothing zero, as all the money will go to the Dogs.

So, by filing these groundless motions by two of the biggest law firms in San Francisco Petitioners counsel became afraid to file an appeal. In addition, Petitioner could not retain another attorney either as every attorney he consulted was afraid that he too would be on the wrong end of a motion for sanctions by Bank of America.

Next, Petitioner filed a motion for discovery. The superior court had ruled in favor of a new claim by Bank of America that a Statute of Limitations barred petitioner's defense. This claim was obviously bogus because Mike Goodall had filed this very case back in 1999 to object to Bank of America being the trustee.

Thirdly, the judge delayed two months in signing the order. This delay of two months by the judge was what put the case over the time limit to file the appeal.

The order was submitted to the judge for signing on July 27, 2012. The judge did not sign it until September 26, 2012.

Next the order that Judge Busch has not been after proper notice and a hearing. Indeed, there has never been a fact hearing in this case. There has never been sworn testimony of any witnesses. There has been no discovery. No documents have been produced. Hastings says that he has lost the trust documents. If you look at the case files you will see that there have been no declarations, no exhibits, no verifications, no findings of facts and conclusions of law.

Neither Bank of America nor Guide Dogs for the Blind have ever filed a brief or a memorandum of law in this case. They have never cited a single case, they have never explained upon what legal grounds or theory of law they are entitled to proceed. They have not even explained what they are even doing appearing in this case as the Goodalls all died more than two years ago. They have no standing to be appearing in this case. Only the contestants, namely Guide Dogs and the legitimate heirs, have standing.

Of immediate concern is the court felt that the appeal from the May 16, 2012 was untimely. However, Petitioner contends that this is not correct because Petitioner was prevented by the actions of opposing counsel and actions of the judge which made it impossible for him to file the appeal any sooner than he did. Indeed, Petitioner waited in the court room for the San Francisco Judge to sign his final order in this case so he could go down to the filing room to file this notice of appeal.

After considering this matter, this court should dismiss this case entirely. The proper Probate Proceeding involving the Goodall Estate is now pending over in Marin County Probate Court. Case No. PR 1100596. Everything about this case happened over in Marin. The only reason Bank of America filed in San Francisco is they do not like the judge over in Marin.

This action by Bank of America should be dismissed and thrown out of court for a deeper reason, which is that Bank of America has never had standing in this case. Bank of America was never the legal trustee of the Goodall Trust.

Kenneth and Rachel Goodall were the trustees. Upon the death of Kenneth, the Trust documents which are annexed as exhibits show that Michael became the co-trustee with his mother and upon her death Michael became the sole trustee. The documents showing this are annexed as exhibits here. At no time did Bank of America have any rights in this case. They simply usurped and stole this case because of the millions of dollars involved.

This document is prepared in Century Schoolbook New Bold 12 point with a word count of 8956 words.

Dated July 15, 2013 Respectfully Submitted,

Samuel H. Sloan
Administrator of Estate of
K. Michael Goodall
with Will Annexed
461 Peachstone Terrace
San Rafael CA 94903
(415) 419-5980
917-659-3397
samhsloan@gmail.com

Court of Appeal, First Appellate District, Division Four - No. A137190

S208895

IN THE SUPREME COURT OF CALIFORNIA

En Banc

BANK OF AMERICA N. A., Plaintiff and Respondent,

v.

SAMUEL H. SLOAN, Objector and Appellant.

The petition for review is denied.

Chin, J., was recused and did not participate.

SUPREME COURT
FILED

APR 17 2013

Frank A. McGuire Clerk

Deputy

CANTIL-SAKAUYE

Chief Justice

IN THE COURT OF APPEAL OF THE STATE OF CALIFORNIA

FIRST APPELLATE DISTRICT

DIVISION FOUR

BANK OF AMERICA N.A.,

Plaintiff and Respondent,

v.

SAMUEL SLOAN,

Objector and Appellant.

A137190

(San Francisco County
Super. Ct. No. PTR99273030)

Appellant Samuel Sloan purports to appeal from a September 27, 2012 order denying his motion for reconsideration.

A court's ruling on a motion for reconsideration is not appealable. (Code Civ Proc. § 1008, subd. (g).)

The appeal is dismissed.

FILED

JAN 15 2013

Court of Appeal - First App. Dist.
DIANA HERBERT
By
DEPUTY

Dated: JAN 15 2013

P

IN THE COURT OF APPEAL OF THE STATE OF CALIFORNIA

FIRST APPELLATE DISTRICT

DIVISION FOUR

BANK OF AMERICA N.A.,

Plaintiff and Respondent,

v.

SAMUEL SLOAN,

Objector and Appellant.

A137190

(San Francisco County
Super. Ct. No. PTR99273030)

BY THE COURT:

Appellant's petition for rehearing, filed on January 29, 2013, is denied.

FILED

FEB - 6 2013

Court of Appeal - First App. Dist.
DIANA HERBERT
By ______________
DEPUTY

Dated: FEB - 6 2013

______________ P.J.

SAM WARE (State Bar No. 105005)
700 Larkspur Landing Circle, #199
Larkspur, CA 94939

Telephone 415-464-4872

E-mail sam@samware.us

Attorney for Sam Sloan,
administrator of Estate
of K. Michael Goodall

SUPERIOR COURT OF THE STATE OF CALIFORNIA

COUNTY OF SAN FRANCISCO

In the Matter of	)	Case No. PTR-99-273030
	)	
The Goodall Trust dated September 12, 1990	)	Declaration of David S. Moore
	)	
	)	Hearing Date: June , 2012
	)	Time:
	)	Department: 204
	/	

David S. Moore declares:

1. I make this declaration based upon my own personal knowledge unless otherwise stated.

2. I am a Forensic Document Examiner. I have a laboratory located at 9010 Barrhill Way, Fair Oaks, California 95628. This laboratory contains highly sophisticated devices such as microscopes that enable me to determine if a document is authentic or not.

3. I have more than thirty years of document and investigative experience, including assignments with the Crime Laboratories of the United States Army, the United States Postal Inspection Service, the Las Vegas Metropolitan Police, and the California Department of Justice. I have received extensive training regarding handwriting identification, ink and document analysis, and examination, reflected in courses from the United States Army, the United States Secret Service, the Federal Bureau of Investigation, the American Academy of Forensic Sciences, and the California Criminalistics Institute. I have been certified as a "Diplomate" of the American Board of Forensic Document Examiners since 1978. From 1999 to 2002, I served as one of the Directors on that Board. I have published numerous articles in the field of forensic document examination in the Journal of Forensic Sciences, including "lie Electrostatic Detection Apparatus (ESDA) and its Effect on Latent Prints on Paper", March 1988; "The Importance of Shading Habits in Handwriting Identification: A Case Study", January 1983; the "Evaluation of a Method to Detect the Site of Rubber Erasures by Powder", October 1981. In addition, I have presented numerous papers at meetings and conferences of the American Academy of Forensic Sciences, the American Society of Questioned Document

Examiners, the International Association of Identification, the Southwestern Association of Forensic Document Examiners, and the Southeastern Association of Forensic Scientists.

4. I have presented numerous classes on questioned document subjects to federal, state and local law enforcement officials, both government and private attorneys, as well as to bank and insurance personnel.

5. I have testified as an expert in the field of questioned documents in justice, municipal, and superior, federal and military courts and administrative hearings in excess of 700 times in more than 20 states throughout the United States, including California.

6. In order to conduct a proper forensic document examination of the original questioned wills and trusts in this instant case, it is my professional opinion that the following tests may be necessary.

a. Visual examination;
b. Microscopic examination;
c. Photographic examination;
d. Ink examination;
e. Handwriting examination;
f. Indentation examination; and
g. Any other non-destructive examination necessary to determine the authenticity of the questioned document.

7. These types of examinations are necessary to evaluate the genuineness of questioned documents. An ink examination allows me to analyze the inks used in the documents and draw conclusions about the use of different inks and to detect whether

alternations and/or interlineations have been made. Indentation examination permits me to draw conclusions about whether certain documents were together when they were originally created and also to ascertain whether there is other information contained on the documents in the form of indentations that may provide insight into when the document was created and under what conditions. The other examinations requested may enable me to draw conclusions about the time frame in which the document was created and about the genuineness of the document.

8. The indentation examination, the ink examination, the fluorescence and luminescence examinations require the use of laboratory equipment. For example, the microscope that he uses is a stereoscopic trinocular microscope that is not readily portable. The video spectral comparator (VSC) that I use for ink evaluation is not readily portable. It is often imperative to strictly control lighting conditions during an examination; this can be done in a laboratory setting, but often cannot be done elsewhere.

9. The various examinations that I have listed and the equipment that I employ during the examination of the questioned documents are routine in cases of this nature. Failure to examine the questioned document in a laboratory setting, with proper instrumentation, may result in loss of valuable evidence that would directly address the issue of the document's authenticity.

10. On May 7, 2012, I conducted a Forensic Document Examination of the wills of Kenneth F. Goodall and Rachel A. Goodall on file at the Marin County Civil Court located at The Civic Center, Hall of Justice, Room 113, San Rafael CA 94901. In this forensic

document examination I was assisted by Irene Mariani, Supervisor in the Civil Department of the Clerk's Office. These wills are on file at the Marin County Superior Court. Kenneth Goodall's will is number W001916 and Rachel Goodall's will is number W001919.

11. I have examined at my office laboratory in Fair Oaks, California a white file folder with a business card of James R. Hastings, Attorney at Law, annexed. This white file folder contains the following documents:

Bill from J. R. Hastings dated July 27, 1994

Bill from J. R. Hastings dated July 20, 1994

Business Card of James R. Hastings

Letter by J. R. Hastings to Kenneth and Rachel Goodall dated July 26, 1994

Assignment of Personal Property from Kenneth and Rachel Goodall to the Goodall Trust undated and unsigned marked COPY

Letter from J. R. Hastings to Christine Clausen of Bank of America dated July 26, 1994 informing B of A that it has been named alternate executor of the Goodall Trust unsigned by Hastings and Kenneth and Rachel Goodall marked COPY

Unsigned Declaration of the Goodall Trust, 37 numbered pages plus one unnumbered page entitled SCHEDULE OF COMMUNITY PROPERTY ASSETS

One Page AMENDMENT TO GOODALL TRUST Preamble unsigned and undated marked COPY with one page unsigned Notary Public acknowledgment by James R. Hastings (This two page document is NOT included in the 1994 Trust as submitted by Bank of America but is stapled on top of the unsigned 1994 trust)

Last Will of Rachel Goodall unsigned

DURABLE POWER OF ATTORNEY FOR MANAGEMENT OR PROPERTY AND PERSONAL AFFAIRS unsigned and marked COPY

DURABLE POWER OF ATTORNEY FOR HEALTH CARE unsigned and Marked COPY

DURABLE POWER OF ATTORNEY FOR MANAGEMENT OR PROPERTY AND PERSONAL AFFAIRS signed original signed by Rachel Goodall accepted by Kenneth Goodall notarized by James R. Hastings on August 24, 1994 in legal blue backing

DURABLE POWER OF ATTORNEY FOR HEALTH CARE signed original by Rachel A. Goodall dated August 24, 1994 witnessed and signed by James R. Hastings and Nancy Rodgers in legal blue backing

A separate document entitled "Employment of J. R. Hastings Law Corporation Estate of Kenneth F. Goodall" dated September 19, 1994 signed by James R. Hastings and Endorsed by Rachel Goodall on SEP 27,

1994

12. I have examined documents contained in as Green Ring Binder that appear to be original documents. The Green Ring Binder includes tab markers. It contains the following signed original documents under these respective tab numbers:

Tab 7: Original Letter from James R. Hastings to Kenneth F. and Rachel Goodall dated September 12, 1990, with original signature by James R. Hastings and pencil notes by Kenneth F. Goodall

Tab 9: Durable Power of Attorney signed by Kenneth F. Goodall dated August 26, 1989 and notarized by James R. Hastings

Tab 10: Contributions of Anatomical Gift dated May 16, 1989 and April 26, 1989, signed by Kenneth F. Goodall witnessed by James R. Hastings

Tab 10: Contributions of Anatomical Gift dated May 16, 1989 signed by Rachel A. Goodall witnessed by James R. Hastings. (This is one of the two original signatures we have of Rachel A. Goodall.)

Tab 11: California Natural Death Act Directive to Physicians dated April 26, 1989 signed by Kenneth F. Goodall witnessed by James R. Hastings

Tab 11: California Natural Death Act Directive to Physicians dated April 26, 1989 signed by Rachel A. Goodall witnessed by James R. Hastings

Tab 11: California Natural Death Act Directive to Physicians dated May 16, 1989 signed by Kenneth F. Goodall, no witnesses.

Tab 12: Durable Power of Attorney on official form signed by Kenneth F. Goodall no date

Tab 14: Personal Affairs Workbook signed on the first page by Kenneth F. Goodall with numerous hand written notes in pencil.

13. I have also examined the following documents which are copies, not originals:

A document entitled "The Goodall Trust" and dated September 12, 1990.

A document entitled "Declaration of the Goodall Trust" and dated August 24, 1994.

A document entitled "Second Amendment to Goodall Trust" and dated January 19, 1999.

14. The conclusions I have reached as a result of these examinations are as follows:

There are no inconsistencies in the signatures of Nancy Rodgers. They were all signed quickly and legibly.

DURABLE POWER OF ATTORNEY FOR MANAGEMENT OR PROPERTY AND PERSONAL AFFAIRS signed original signed by Rachel Goodall accepted by Kenneth F.

Goodall was signed with two different blue pens. This is not inconsistent with the view that Kenneth F. Goodall was hospitalized at the time and that he and his wife Rachel Goodall signed this document at different times and places.

The document entitled AMENDMENT TO THE GOODALL TRUST as filed in San Francisco Probate Court is a copy of a FAX. The FAX markings show it was sent on Faxed at November 24, 2008 at 12:31 PM One can see fax markings and lines all across the page. Needless to say in a FAXed document the same kind of ink will be used throughout the document. The quality of the signatures are extremely poor and much is illegible. This is a case of GIGO or "Garbage in and Garbage Out".For these reasons, I will need to see the original to determine if these are valid signatures. I am neutral on the question of whether these are authentic signatures.

I declare under penalty of perjury under the laws of the state of California that the foregoing is true and correct.

Date: ______________________________

David S. Moore

SAM WARE (State Bar No. 105005)
700 Larkspur Landing Circle, #199
Larkspur, CA 94939

Telephone 415-464-4872

E-mail sam@samware.us

Attorney for Sam Sloan,
administrator of Estate
of K. Michael Goodall

SUPERIOR COURT OF THE STATE OF CALIFORNIA

COUNTY OF SAN FRANCISCO

In the Matter of the	) Case No. PTR-99-) 273030))
Trust for Michael created under the Goodall Trust dated September 12, 1990	) Declaration of Nancy) Rogers))
	) Hearing Date:) February 8, 2012) Time:) Department: 204 /

Nancy Rogers declares:

1. I make this declaration based upon my own personal knowledge unless otherwise stated.

2. I reside at 470 Peachstone Terrace, San Rafael, CA 94903 and have resided there since before 1964.

3. I have examined the attached copies of the purported Last Will of Kenneth F. Goodall, attached hereto as Exhibit A, and the purported Last Will of Rachel A Goodall, attached hereto as Exhibit B.

4. At page 7 of each of these Exhibits, I see what purports to be my signature as a witness to those wills, along with James R Hastings as the other witness, purportedly executed on August 24, 1994 in San Rafael California.

5. Although the signatures there appears to be mine, I do not recall ever acting as a witness to any will for either Kenneth Goodall or Rachel Goodall at any time, and I am sure that I would remember having done so.

6. I do recall that at some time that Rachel Goodall asked me and Barbara Dagitz, another of our neighbors, to be the two witnesses to a legal document pertaining to Rachel Goodall, which I recall being a health care directive or similar document, but never any will at any time.

7. I do not recall ever witnessing any signing of any document by Kenneth Goodall at any time, though I do remember quite clearly my husband and I visiting him in his home shortly before his death.

I declare under penalty of perjury under the laws of the state of California that the foregoing is true and correct.

Date: ______________________

Declaration of Nancy Rogers

Don A. Lesser (SBN #112887)
THE LESSER LAW GROUP
1010 B Street, Suite 300
San Rafael, California 94901
Telephone: (415) 453-7600
Facsimile: (415)295-4122
Email: Dlesser@LesserGroup.com
Attorney for Subpoenaed Witness
JAMES R HASTINGS

CALIFORNIA SUPERIOR COURT
SAN FRANCISCO COUNTY

-----,---------- .. --------

Case No. PTR-99-273030

In the Matter of the Trust for Michael created under the Goodall Trust dated January 19, 1999

DECLARATION OF JAMES R. HASTINGS PURSUANT TO COURT ORDER ON RESPONDENTS MOTION TO COMPEL PRODUCTION OF DOCUMENTS AND FURTHER DEPOSITION

Hearing: January 12, 2012
Time: 2:15 p.m.
Department: 204

BY FAX

I, James R Hastings, declare as follows:

1. I am an attorney at law licensed to practice in the State of California. I provide this declaration ill response to this Court's order on Respondent's Motion to Compel Production of Documents and Further Deposition. The following facts are personally known to me. If called upon to do so, I could and would testify competently to them.

2. This declaration describes my further search for my Estate Planning file relating to Kenneth and Rachel Goodall, following my November 14,2011 deposition in this matter. Since then, I have re-examined the two groups of files I have at my home. As the number of the file I am looking for begins with the letter "G," I looked at every "G" file in those files at my home and did not find the Goodells' file, I also looked in both storage areas at my office, active and inactive, again looking at every "G" file. and again found nothing. I also looked at all of the Goodall files retained in an armoire near my assistant's work area, which contains "active" files, and still found nothing. I have searched my entire office, where I prepared the declarations I have submitted in this matter. Previously I inquired of all of the staff people who work in my office when and where they last saw the file, and no one could recall.

3. I have not knowingly discarded or destroyed the file, or instructed anyone else to do so, nor have I knowingly given it to anyone else. At this point, I have searched everywhere I can think of where the file might be found.

I declare under penalty of perjury under the laws of the State of California that the foregoing is true and. correct and that this declaration was executed this 1 day of February, 2012 at San Rafael. California.

James R. Hastings

DECLARATION OF JAMES R. HASTINGS PURSUANT TO COURT ORDER ON RESPONDENT'S MOTION TO COMPEL PRODUCTION OF DOCUMENTS AND FURTHER DEPOSITION CASE NO. PTR-99-273030

Made in the USA
Monee, IL
04 November 2026

67375836R00036